Disowned

A Twentieth-Century Jew and His Experience With Jesus

Steve Cohen

A Purple Pomegranate Book
Purple Pomegranate Productions, 80 Page Street,
San Francisco, CA 94102

Steve Cohen is chief of station for the Jews for Jesus
branch in Ft. Lauderdale, Florida.

Disowned

Published by Purple Pomegranate Productions,
80 Page Street, San Francisco, CA 94102
Purple Pomegranate Productions is a division of Jews for Jesus.
If you desire to reprint all or any portion of this book, please write to
Permissions, 60 Haight Street, San Francisco, CA 94102.

Cover design by Sue Saunders

95 96 97 98 99 00 01 9 8 7 6 5 4 3 2 1

Printed in the United States of America
ISBN 1-881022-20-X

Many flowery words would never adequately express the love I have for my father and mother, so I will simply say, "This is dedicated to dad and mom, Robert and Barbara Cohen. Mother, may you be comforted by God in your solitude after dad's death in 1990."

I am eternally grateful to Alan and Kathy Rither. Because of their faithful prayers, testimony and witness, I have begun my spiritual journey in Y'shua.

I give thanks to God for my wife Jan. She has done an excellent job mothering our five children: Micha, Sarah, Noah, Seth and Elizabeth. Her faithfulness is a blessing and her many sacrifices have helped make possible our involvement with Jews for Jesus.

When I first asked Ruth Rosen if she would be willing to help me out with the writing of this book, I am not sure that she knew how big of a help she would be to me and to this project. Thank you Ruth for giving so selflessly. And also, a big thank you to Janet Reed whose copyediting was terrific. And, of course, to Steve Lawson for bringing this to print!

Finally, I praise God for Moishe Rosen's leadership, steadfastness and encouragement to me. In 1976, Moishe told me, "All I have to give is an opportunity." I continue to see the opportunity to serve. Thank you for making this book possible through Jews for Jesus.

—Steve Cohen, March 1995

Robert Cohen pictured in one of the few photos Steve Cohen has of his father.

Jan and Steve Cohen

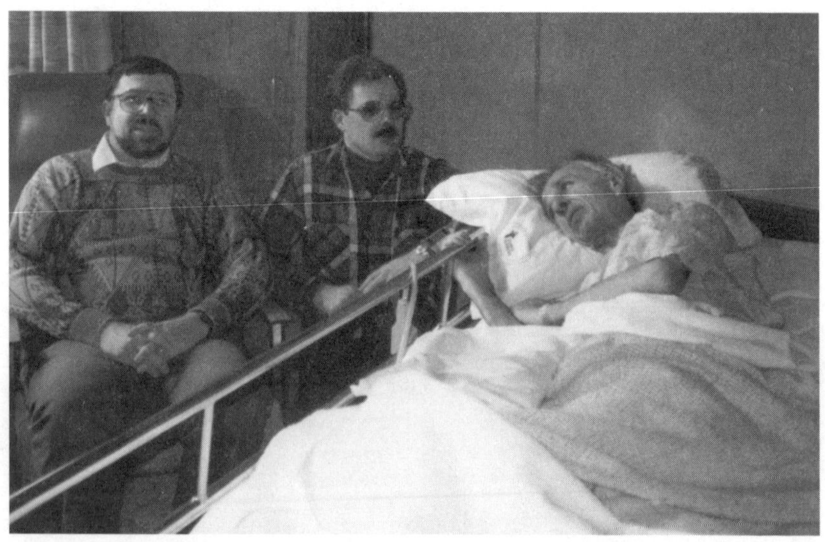

Steve Cohen and his brother, Dennis, visit their critically ill father.

I had just been accepted into law school and was contemplating my move to Tacoma, Washington. Dry days are rare in the Pacific Northwest; yet, I was standing on a sunny Seattle hillside overlooking Lake Washington when a big black Lincoln Continental pulled up within a few feet of me. A man in a dark suit emerged and strode purposefully toward me. I had never seen him before nor have I seen him since. He informed me that he had a message for me. A message, he said, from God: ***"You are to study the Bible and become a believer in Jesus because your mission in life is to bring the gospel to other Jewish people."***

His message delivered, he turned, walked back to his car and before I could answer, he drove away. I was certain he must be *meshugge* (Yiddish for crazy). First, he didn't know me. Second, my "mission," if you could call it that, was to become a lawyer. Third, and most important, who ever heard of a Jewish person believing in Jesus? Certainly not I!

My name is Steve Cohen, and despite what I once considered a ridiculous notion, I am a Jew who eventually decided to be, most definitely, for Jesus. Let me tell you my story.

I grew up in Pasco, a small town in eastern Washington. My parents owned a jewelry store, but lest you begin picturing wealthy ladies and gentlemen poring over glittering gold and gem-studded trinkets, let me tell you that our store was a far cry from Tiffany's. In fact, it was difficult for my folks to keep the small business afloat. I helped out at the store, and though money was scarce, perhaps we *were* "well off" because our financial struggle was a family affair.

We were not strict in practicing the Jewish religion, but my parents did their best to rear my brother, Dennis, and me with high moral standards. The nearest Reform temple, Beth El, was about half an hour away in Richland. The nearest rabbi was in Seattle, a five-hour drive. My parents were not willing to invest the time to take us back and forth, so we grew up with little biblical knowledge. Still, we were unquestionably Jews.

Pasco was no place to shop for traditional Jewish foods, but occasionally we ordered "care packages" that Brenner Brothers Deli bussed in from Seattle. We treasured the salami, the pastrami, the rye bread and the lox, savoring every bite. Of course at Passover, there was matzoh (unleavened bread), which we didn't exactly savor but were glad to have because it was a link to our people and our heritage. One compensation for a week without regular bread was the delicious matzoh brie (matzoh dipped in beaten eggs and fried like French toast—we smothered ours with fresh strawberry jam). But for those who know New York, Zabar's it wasn't.

My parents found other ways to reinforce our Jewish identity. In particular, my father was careful to teach me that our people have suffered much persecution in the past and that he wasn't going to tolerate prejudice in the present. I vividly recall the time he took to task the manager of a department store across the street from our family store. The man had derided our people terribly, and Dad, normally one to avoid confrontation, stood up to him in my presence. Dad helped me realize the importance of taking pride in our heritage. I grew up feeling proud of what our people had accomplished and contributed to society; yet, I wondered about religion.

I recall watching the Billy Graham crusades on television. I loved to listen to George Beverly Shea sing, and I admired Dr. Graham for the moral lessons he brought. However, as soon as he began inviting people to commit their lives to Jesus, I switched channels. I knew that was not for me, since I was Jewish. I didn't have much knowledge of my own religion, but I did know that I was not supposed to believe someone else's!

It bothered me that I didn't know more about Judaism, and I sensed that something was missing in my life. When I was sixteen years old, I lashed out at my mother, blaming her and my father for the void where I thought my religious background ought to be. Why else would I feel empty inside? I generally excelled at whatever I put my head and hands to—I was first chair clarinetist at each level of school, first on the tennis team and always on the honor roll. Yet, I wasn't satisfied and reasoned that it must be God or religion that was missing from my life. My mother's response was, "In two years you'll go away to college. Then you can get all the religion you want."

My grandparents made it possible for me to attend college, and I chose the University of Washington. I hadn't the foggiest idea of what to do with my life—I went to college because it was the thing to do, and I felt that I was expected to go.

My father told me that he had joined a Jewish fraternity when he was in college and suggested that it would be good for me to join one, too. I pledged Zeta Beta Tau, imagining the house would provide some of the religious experience I had missed in my upbringing. I was dismayed to find myself in the midst of a close-knit group of friends who already knew one another and were geared for social, not spiritual, interaction.

One of my closer friends at the fraternity was Ken Packhouse. Neither of us enjoyed gambling into the early morning hours or the partying that typified most fraternities, including ours. When I recall how much Ken and I seemed to have in common, it seems ironic how our paths eventually and radically diverged. After graduation, he went to Israel and became a scholar at a Jewish organization called "Aish Ha Torah," while I—well, even I would not have believed the path I would one day follow.

I spent the summer of 1968 in Dusseldorf, Germany. I could speak German, having studied the language since ninth grade, and my grandmother had ties to the "old country." I worked the first half of the summer at a chemical plant called Henkel, a job I got through a student exchange program. I spent the rest of the summer hitchhiking throughout Europe, visiting famous synagogues and cathedrals during my journey. It was quite an adventure, especially the day that the Soviet Union invaded Czechoslovakia. I was in a youth hostel in Copenhagen at the time, as were many Czechoslovakian people for whom the invasion was reminiscent of World War II.

I returned to Seattle in time for the fall term and the Jewish High Holidays. I accepted the invitation of a fraternity brother to attend services with his family. When his mother asked me how I'd spent my summer, I described my adventures. She almost had a heart attack! She was a Holocaust survivor, and the mention of Germany stirred up traumatic memories of the Nazi regime. "How could you go to *that* country and work with *those* people?" she shrieked. I couldn't believe that a fellow Jew would treat me as though I'd somehow been responsible for the horrors of the Holocaust— simply because I didn't share her hatred of all German people.

The Holocaust is an atrocity with which all of my people are familiar to some extent. In fact, I chose to give a speech about it in my public speaking class. We all were assigned a ten-minute speech on the subject of our choice, and I had decided on anti-Semitism for my topic. I went down to the local chapter of the B'nai B'rith Anti Defamation League to do some research. There I saw the anti-Semitic statements Martin Luther made in his 1543 treatise, *On the Jews and Their Lies.*

My speech was a clumsily crafted attempt to show how *"so-called* Christians" were the main perpetrators of hatred against my people. I was excruciatingly nervous as I picked up a piece of chalk and drew a large cross on the blackboard. Then I carefully added lines perpendicular to each arm of the cross, creating a swastika intended to illustrate my point as I pronounced my judgment, "What Luther began in 1543, Hitler tried to finish in 1943." I continued my speech in what seemed to be the longest ten minutes of my life. I was so nervous in front of those twelve classmates that I decided I would *never* be a public speaker!

Meanwhile, my second year of fraternity life proved to be no better than the first. Our house seemed to differ from the others only inasmuch as we served no pork and our grade point averages were generally higher. I found next to nothing of God there. Disillusioned, I moved out of the fraternity house and into an apartment with a friend named Will.

By that time, I had set a goal: I would become a criminal attorney. However, I had to take a slight detour in pursuing my goal because the Vietnam War was raging and my draft number was low. I did not want to join the military, nor did I want to be drafted. I enjoyed airplanes and flying, so in 1970 I enlisted in the Air Force Reserves, hoping to qualify for flight school. I didn't know that 20/20 vision was required, and I failed to qualify on that basis.

So what was available? The only opening at the time was aircraft maintenance. I didn't know the proper side of a wrench or screwdriver, much less how to repair aircraft. Nevertheless, I took the position, as it seemed to offer the least amount of danger, while allowing me to continue the pursuit of my goals.

I was inducted in April of 1970 and went to Lackland Air Force Base in San Antonio, Texas for basic training. There I met Alan Rither, a graduate of the University of Washington, a lawyer—and a Christian. We became fast friends during basic training and purposed to maintain that friendship back in Seattle. Then came technical school training. I was assigned to Sheppherd Air Force Base in Wichita Falls, Texas, for a course in the basics of aircraft maintenance on the C-130 turbo prop airplane.

After the thirteen hottest weeks of a Texas summer, I returned to Seattle where I was assigned to McCord Air Force Base in Tacoma for Reserve duty. Once we returned to Seattle, we were obligated to attend one weekend a month and two weeks during the summer. Ironically, there were no C-130s assigned to our base. I would watch the C-141s come in, but there was little I could do other than help guide aircraft to the appropriate "parking spot." I recall sitting in the cockpit many Saturdays that fall, listening to University of Washington Huskies' football games on the pilot's headphones.

Alan and I continued our friendship as we had planned, and he had a built-in opportunity to speak with me about Jesus at least once a month. We'd usually have lunch together, and I'd listen politely when he spoke of his faith. I was interested to learn what he, as a Gentile, thought about God and the Bible. I didn't take anything he said personally, figuring his beliefs were fine for him but had nothing to do with me, a Jew.

One day Alan invited me to his home. The first thing I saw was a painted brass ornament hanging on his door. It was a greeting: "Shalom, peace to all who enter here." I was impressed and was even more so when I walked into his apartment and sensed just how peaceful it really was. There truly *was* something different about him. I intuitively knew that his "something" was what I had been missing since I was a teen.

When Alan began to tell me about Jesus, I tried to deflect the conversation to something with which I felt more conversant: cosmology, the study of the universe.

I had spent the last two years of my undergraduate work as an assistant to Professor Stuart Carter Dodd, a true genius. I immersed myself in his pantheistic theory of the universe that he laid out so masterfully, but little did I comprehend the implications of his theory! Professor Dodd's main premise was that the "stuff" of the universe is constantly and randomly evolving and devolving into different levels of organization.

Alan listened patiently as I plodded through "facts," theories and mathematical equations ad nauseam. Finally, Alan broadsided me with a question I had never asked myself during all my studies, "Where did all the stuff in the universe come from, anyway?"

I had never questioned the presumption that the "stuff" had always existed. Alan pointed out that Professor Dodd had deified matter rather than acknowledging the existence of the Creator. He also challenged me to see that the intricate design of the universe belied the theory of random interaction leading to higher levels of organization. I found myself thinking that it took more faith to accept Dodd's ideas than to accept the fact that there is a God who created the universe.

During this time when I was rethinking and beginning to search, I was involved in another kind of search as well. I was single—and looking for a life partner. I had no idea how abruptly that search would end.

On February 24, 1971, I went on my very first, and last, blind date. My roommate, Will, had a girlfriend, Kate, who had a roommate: Janice Anne Isbell. Jan was my blind date, and before she said a single word, I knew she was going to be my wife. After our date, I think she knew, too. Will and Kate eventually broke up, but Jan and I were together to stay. Two years later we married.

In the interim, August of 1972, I was accepted into law school in Tacoma, Washington. The day before I moved to Tacoma, I was standing out on a sunny Seattle hillside overlooking Lake Washington and the university district. It was then that the big black Lincoln Continental drove up, and a stranger approached me. His dark suit might as well have been a Western

Union uniform, because he politely delivered his message then left, his purpose apparently accomplished. He did not attempt to explain the message that he claimed God had for me: *"You are to study the Bible and become a believer in Jesus because your mission in life is to bring the gospel to other Jewish people."* It was too bizarre for me to try to correct him, and I certainly was not going to tell a total stranger that he must've gotten his wires crossed because I intended to be a lawyer.

Meanwhile, Alan continued to pray for me and tell me about Jesus on our Reserve weekends. We would sit together and discuss what had happened in the preceding month. I told him of my struggles with law school. He responded by taking out his pocket Bible and reading verses that were meaningful to him. He always managed to bring the conversation back to Jesus. Frankly, I did not know enough about the Bible to counter him. I wanted to be around Alan because, while I felt overcome by life's difficulties, he seemed able to overcome them. He had finished law school, and I was in my first year. We both were in the Air Force Reserves, a situation that involved its own set of quirks and challenges. He was newly married, and while Jan and I were not yet wed, we had committed to one another with a view toward marriage. Through everything, Alan radiated joy amid adversity, while the same sorts of adversity made me downright grumpy.

I could no longer dismiss what he was saying as having nothing to do with me, and perhaps for that reason, I started to challenge his beliefs. When that had little effect, I finally told him, "I'm Jewish. Jewish people don't believe, nor do we need to believe in Jesus!" I assumed that would be enough to stop him from talking to me about God, but I had no idea that he would continue talking to God about me!

Alan later admitted that he had prayed daily for God to make me miserable in what he described as my spiritual complacency so that I would have to consider whether Y'shua (the Jewish way to say Jesus) was the promised Messiah.

In December of 1972, two months before our wedding, Jan's parents invited us to spend the holidays with them in Grand Coulee, Washington. They asked me to join them at their church for a Christmas Eve candlelight service. I had never been to a church before, but I certainly didn't want to offend my future in-laws, so I agreed to come. With no idea what to expect, I sat in the very back row.

The service began at 11:00 P.M. We each received a small candle with a bit of paper wrapped around it to prevent hot wax from burning our hands. The service was a strange new experience for me, but there were some familiar elements. I'd sung some of the carols for the annual Christmas program when I was in grade school. Later, in high school and college, these same carols were standard fare for the concerts we gave. Still, I felt out of place. After all, this was *their* holiday, not mine.

Jan's mother led the choir, and Jan and her sister sang a lovely duet. At the end of the service, all electrical lights were extinguished. The only point of light to break the darkness of the sanctuary was a small candle burning brightly on the altar. The pastor invited the whole congregation to stand with him in a circle. He lit his candle from the altar and shared that fire with those standing near him. As the fire was passed from one person to the next, I was touched by the warmth, the glow, the joy that was so evident in that place. But I remained in the back, hidden in darkness.

I continued "in the dark" for some time, and in May of 1973, when I got my grades, God answered Alan's prayers that I be shaken out of my complacency. *I had failed! Flunked out of law school!* What a blow! I was at a complete loss, for I had invested so much of the previous three years toward my goal of law school, and that goal had vanished into thin air. Why?

One evening in late May, I was looking out my bedroom window where a lantern shone brightly in the backyard. I thought to myself or to whomever might be listening: "If there really is a God, prove it! Make that light in the backyard go out." *Poof!* The light was extinguished in an instant. Well, we were in the midst of a thunderstorm, so I reasoned that it was just a coincidence. Nevertheless, I waited about five minutes and then thought, "OK, if you're really there, make it come back on." Immediately, light from the lantern pierced the darkness. I was floored and asked for no more signs that night!

That weekend, Jan and I went to several garage sales in the area, and I bought a small Bible for $3.00. It was bound in white leather and looked like a Bible that might have been given to someone as a wedding gift. I didn't realize at the time that God was wooing me.

I began reading the Gospel of Matthew—my very first foray into the New Testament. From the first page, I discovered what no one, not even Alan, had ever told me: *Jesus was Jewish!* He attended synagogue, read the Hebrew Scriptures, celebrated the Sabbath, Passover and the other festivals—*and he was speaking to Jewish people about the God of Abraham, Isaac and Jacob!*

I was impressed. Still, everything I knew about my religion and my upbringing warned me that I was on dangerous ground as I could *not* be

11

Jewish and believe in Jesus.

The next six months seemed to be the worst of my life. I could not seem to do anything right. I went through six jobs in those six months, and after losing each job, I had to tell Jan the bad news. It was as if the rug were being pulled out from under my life.

Alan invited me to hear the attorney general for the state of California address a large group of men during a lunch hour. I went because I still had an interest in law, but he was not there to speak about our legal system. He came to tell about God's justice system—how He offered atonement for sin though death of the Messiah, Jesus. I stayed for lunch, but I was nervous being around all those Christians. As soon as the attorney general finished speaking, I left as quickly as I could. The presence of the Lord was so real—I couldn't take it. I was confronted with my own sin and need for forgiveness, but I didn't want to yield. It was becoming more and more difficult for me to dismiss Jesus.

Jan was the organist at a church in Tacoma. I attended some of the inquirer's classes and asked some rather obnoxious questions as I tried to challenge the others' faith. They responded with kindness.

Alan kept sending books to read, tracts to consider and tapes to hear, *and* he kept praying for me. Once he asked me, if the promised Messiah of Israel were standing right in front of me, how would I recognize him? After all, there have been many false Messiahs throughout history, and even in our day there are a couple who have been hailed as the Messiah: Rev. Syung Young Moon, the head of the Unification Church, and Menachem Schneerson, the former head of the Lubavitch sect of Judaism.

I knew that the Messiah had to fulfill certain prophecies, and Alan's question made me realize that I was ignorant of those prophecies. I could not make a case for or against Jesus as a false Messiah if I didn't acquaint myself with the evidence that would prove the identity of the true Messiah. If I learned those prophecies, God would make it clear to me whether I ought to follow or reject this Jesus. I dug into the Jewish Bible and explored the case Alan had been making for Jesus as the Messiah. I found I could not rule out Jesus!

Now it seemed I was worse off than before. By December of 1973, I was battling with what seemed indisputable evidence for the messiahship of Jesus. It would turn my life upside down if I accepted what the Scriptures seemed to indicate, but on the other hand, if I rejected what was true, I would be going against God.

On December 23, 1973, Alan and his wife, Kathy, came to our home for dinner. Alan brought with him a couple of cassette tapes of the testimony of a Jewish believer named Art Katz. He previously had given me Art's book, *Ben Israel*. I had found the written testimony extremely challenging, and as the four of us listened to the tapes, I was more convinced than ever that Jesus was truly my Messiah. Alan told me that he wanted to know for certain that I would spend eternity with him, so he extended me a personal invitation to receive God's gift of eternal life.

Instantly the battle intensified. Doubts flooded my mind even as a sense of peace flooded my heart. I glanced around the room and my eyes fell on the two candles burning in our living room. The darkness and light were vivid reminders of that candlelight service, when from the darkness in the back of the church, I'd witnessed the joy of those lighting their small candles. I remembered the night of the thunderstorm and how God seemed to provide me with a sign from the streetlight. I remembered, too, that Jesus was said to be the light of the world. So I took a bold step. I asked God for one more confirmation. *"If you really want me to follow Jesus as my Messiah, make one of the two candles go out,"* I silently prayed. Alan immediately rose from his chair, walked over to the candles, blew one out and returned to his chair.

The battle was over, yet I had no idea of the battle that was ahead. All I knew was that at 11:20 P.M., the moment of my repentance and commitment to Christ, I experienced a peace I had never known before. It was the same peace that I saw radiate from Alan's face. I keep a picture taken that night in my Bible. It reminds me of God's faithfulness in the midst of my stubbornness and self-centeredness. A year later, I learned that even as I had asked God for yet more proof, Kathy was also praying, "Lord, Steve needs a sign. I don't know what it is, but please give him that sign so he knows this is for real."

But what does a Jew who believes in Jesus do? The next night was Christmas Eve 1973. Jan and I went to the church where she was organist. Again, it was a candlelight service. This time, I sat right up in front. The pastor, Rev. Robert Anderson, invited Jan and me to his home for a late supper after the service. We cheerfully accepted.

A whole new world started opening up to me. I attended the new believer's class where I asked questions, *lots* of questions. I felt I had so much catching up to do. A couple of weeks after I came to faith in Jesus, I was sitting in Sunday school, asking the rest of the class, "How do you begin to tell others about Jesus? How do you tell them what He means to you?"

I was astonished when a woman who had been a member of that congregation for years stood up and declared, "I am a Lutheran, and we don't do that sort of thing," and then she sat down! How could this be? If Jesus is the Messiah, then we needed to tell everyone about Him.

I've since learned that she was not speaking for all Lutherans. Yet, over the years, I have also learned that Jews are not the only people who have to break with tradition in order to follow Y'shua. Many Christians need to break with their tradition of *not* sharing their faith in order to obey Jesus' command:

> All authority has been given to me in heaven and on earth. Go therefore and make disciples of all the nations, baptizing them in the name of the Father and of the Son and of the Holy Spirit, teaching them to observe all the things that I have commanded you; and lo, I am with you always, even to the end of the age. (Matthew 28:18-20)

All who are followers of Y'shua should be committed to carrying out that Great Commission to the end that others will come to know what we have discovered: Jesus really is the Messiah promised long ago. There is so very much at stake—eternal separation for those who are outside of Christ.

As I continued to grow in my faith, I had many more questions about the Bible. One day I asked Pastor Anderson about Jonah and the whale (or Behemoth as some call it). His next comment startled me: "Well, we don't believe that actually happened. This is simply a story to give us moral guidance. We don't have to take everything in the Bible literally."

I was profoundly disturbed by that. "If we don't take the Jonah text literally, where do we draw the line?" I argued, "Couldn't one extend this line of reasoning and conclude that the resurrection never happened?" But as kind and gracious as that pastor was, he was not going to change his views of Scripture because of the questions of a new believer.

I was sad, because I knew that I would be leaving that congregation sooner or later. It turned out to be sooner, as Jan received an invitation to become organist at another church in Tacoma. The pastor, Gary Grafwallner, was creative, outgoing, young at heart and had a real desire for people to know the vitality of a personal relationship with God. Through the grace of God, I grew in my faith and knowledge of Scripture. Jan and I started taking Hebrew lessons at a local synagogue. In order to keep up with it, I offered a beginner's class to the members of the church. I kept a couple of weeks ahead of them as we worked our way through the first chapter of Genesis.

I also frequented a local Christian bookstore. The owner had befriended me and helped me see the wide range of reading possibilities. I gravitated toward the reference books like the biblical dictionaries, but Jan and I were living on very limited resources, so most of the time I was "just looking." I began to wonder if there were any other Jews who believed in Jesus, so I left my name at the bookstore and asked the manager to let me know if she could put me in touch with any.

In the spring of 1974, I contracted pneumonia and was housebound for six weeks. Day after day, my main event was navigating down the long flight of stairs to get our mail, then struggling back up the stairs in order to crawl back into bed. I had no energy for anything except reading, and read I did. The Lord used those six weeks to immerse me in His Word, which I drank in with increasing thirst. Each page filled me with the joy of knowing Him and a realization of the responsibility imparted along with that knowledge. Just as I was well enough to get out of the house, I received more reading material from an unexpected source.

A woman named Gina Brewington had been visiting Christian bookstores with a recently published work, *Jews for Jesus*. The store owner gave Gina my name and number, and the next thing I knew, she was at my door with a copy of the book in hand.

That book introduced me to a band of Jewish ex-hippies and antiwar dissenters who believed in Jesus. I was astonished to read how they turned tactics once used to protest against the establishment into tools to proclaim the gospel. They told about Jesus out on the city streets with a lively style of gospel literature. They sang newly written Jewish gospel music, and they used drama to preach on busy street corners. Moishe Rosen was the founder of the group, and he did not retreat from those who opposed its message.

My admiration was due in part to the fact that I had learned from my father to avoid conflict at all costs. I remember a visit from my *Oma* (grandmother) and how she told Dad that the couch would look better "over there." He moved it. When he was making his delicious lentil soup, she complained that it was usually too salty, so he used less salt, contrary to his own tastes. Then *Oma's* visit was over. Dad moved the couch back, and the next time he made the soup, he added the usual amount of salt. Dad hated confrontation and avoided it by compromising whenever possible. That may have been acceptable in dealing with couches and soup, but I gathered from this book that when it came to proclaiming the gospel, compromising is not an option. Far too much is at stake!

Soon after she'd given me the book, Gina called to inform me that Moishe Rosen was coming to Seattle for a speaking engagement. I told her I would be there. Moishe had several people with him, and I was in a room with other Jewish believers in Jesus for the very first time.

They showed slides of the first Jews for Jesus New York City Summer Witnessing Campaign. I saw colorfully clad people who were performing street theater. I saw what appeared to be a birthday party for one of the campaigners—in the form of a parade down Fifth Avenue! The song written for that occasion became the standard birthday song among Jews for Jesus staff (sung to the tune of "L'chaim" from *Fiddler on the Roof*):

> Today is Martha's birthday, to Martha we wish a long life (long life!)
> Not only was she born back then, but she's been born again—
> Praise Y'shua for life.
>
> All the prophets have foretold us that the
> Son would come to set His people free
> So Y'shua came among us so that we could live
> throughout eternity. What's today?
>
> Today is Martha's birthday, to Martha we wish a long life
> Not only was she born back then, but she's been born again
> Praise Y'shua—for life!

The more I saw, the more I felt that these outspoken and seemingly uninhibited people were doing something I admired, but something that was definitely not for me. Yet, I recalled the messenger on the hill who had told me that my mission in life was to bring the gospel to other Jewish people. For the first time I wondered, could it be true?

A few months later, Gina phoned yet again to inform me that the Liberated Wailing Wall was coming to Tacoma. This was the first Jews for Jesus "mobile evangelistic team." They present Jewish gospel music, drama and testimonies. Jan and I fell in love with the music. After the presentation, the team requested that anyone traveling to eastern Washington contact them, as one of the members needed a ride to see some friends that weekend. Well, it was Thanksgiving weekend, and we'd planned to see Jan's parents in Grand Coulee, Washington, so we offered to help. Steffi Geiser, our two small dogs, Jan and I piled into our tiny Fiat 128, and off we went. Steffi told us about the very beginnings of the ministry and invited me to come to California and see what was happening for myself. I couldn't go because I was working in a photography studio. Three weeks later, the owner decided to close the store, and once again, I was out of work.

Being in the Air Force Reserves, I could fly anywhere that military aircraft went for free, as long as there was space available. There were regular flights between Tacoma and Alameda Naval Air Station in Oakland (less than an hour's drive from the Jews for Jesus office). I put on my uniform, went to the base, hopped a DC-9 military hospital plane, and about two hours later, I was in California.

My parents were living in Reno, so I thought I would take a quick excursion to see them. When I called and told them where I was and what I was doing, however, they told me I was not welcome to visit them. They were definitely displeased with my new faith.

Susan Perlman and Tuvya Zaretsky drove me to the Jews for Jesus office, which at that time was just north of San Francisco in a suburb called San Rafael.

Tuvya took me to lunch, and I asked him how his family responded to his faith. I began to realize that the joy we have in our Messiah is neither understood nor shared by our families who don't yet know Him. I had no idea of the storm that was building in my family, but the week I spent in San Francisco was pivotal in my life. I met vibrant Jewish believers who had dedicated themselves to making a difference for the kingdom of God. They were delivering a straightforward gospel message to Jews and Gentiles, regardless of pressure to keep quiet about their faith.

In 1975, there was very little Jewish Christian fellowship in the Seattle area. Jan and I reasoned that if we wanted a gathering, perhaps others did also. We convened our own fellowship group in the home of Dr. Richard and Polly Perkins. They lived sixty miles away from our Tacoma home, but it was worth the drive to meet with other Jewish believers. The fellowship group allowed us to help one another grow in our faith, understand our Jewish heritage and encourage one another to be witnesses to our unsaved friends and family. That little group of fifteen to twenty people continued for many years after we left the Seattle area.

I had a tremendous desire and concern for my family to know Jesus. In June of 1975, I drove to Spokane, Washington to see my brother, Dennis. He listened intently as I explained the gospel to him. Art Katz, the Jewish Christian whose testimony had been so helpful to me, was speaking at Gonzaga University that evening, and Dennis accepted my invitation to hear him. After the meeting was over, my brother went up to speak with Art—and he came back a new believer in Jesus! What I wrestled with for two years, my brother received in just two hours.

My Aunt Jo believed that all roads lead to God and wondered why we would be so exclusive as to say that Jesus is the **only** way. My paternal grandmother asked, "So, am I supposed to call you Monsignor now?" As for my parents, they thought my faith was simply a fad. Just as people tire of clothing and hair styles, they expected me to tire of my "new religion."

I continued to have contact with the staff of Jews for Jesus between 1974 and 1976. At one point, Moishe Rosen came to Portland, Oregon and I drove down to see him. When I arrived at his hotel, he invited me to accompany him to the airport, where he handed me a stack of broadsides (Jews for Jesus-style gospel tracts), pointed to a place of high pedestrian flow and asked me to hand out the pamphlets to whomever would take them.

I had done this a couple of times before and enjoyed seeing people take and read the literature. Then a uniformed airport patrol officer approached me. He had a gun and a badge, and seemed to be twice my size. He asked if I had a permit to hand out the literature. I knew that I was out of my league, so I responded, "I'm here with someone else. He is in charge." Then I went to tell Moishe what had happened.

He gave me the option of standing with him and continuing to hand out the literature side by side, or standing nearby as an observer. He calmly explained that if I continued to hand out the literature, I would probably be arrested. I had no idea what being arrested entailed or how long I might be detained. What would I say to my boss—*I can't come in for work because I was arrested for handing out Christian literature in the Portland airport?* I chose to observe.

I watched as the guard confronted Moishe, who stood his ground until he was told that he was under arrest. Then he left peacefully with the officer…shackled in handcuffs. They took him to a holding area and released him a while later. Eventually the ACLU took the case and lost. Another group from the ACLU represented his appeal and won. That Portland airport arrest became a foundational building block in case law that eventually led to a unanimous Supreme Court decision in another case upholding freedom of speech. That decision ruled in favor of Avi Snyder, a Jews for Jesus branch leader who was arrested for handing out tracts at the Los Angeles International Airport.

I had lost out on a chance at making case law because I backed down in Portland. I never forgot that lesson during my five different arrests, which took place much later in Toronto and Boston. But those stories are for another time.

In 1976, Jan and I applied to serve as full-time missionaries. We were accepted and we began *the* adventure of our lifetime. My maternal grandmother met with Jan and me just after we joined the missionary staff. Not one to beat around the bush, she asked, "So nu, how much are they going to pay you?" Well, back then, we had a *combined* income of $800 a month, plus mileage for the van. When she heard that, her jaw dropped. "But that is less than the rent I pay on my apartment," she said. "How are you going to live?"

But I could respond with a cheerful smile: "Don't worry, *Oma*, God is going to take care of us!" Little did she know that two years later we would return to visit her, and she would be astonished by our joy and peace and how God indeed had taken care of us. At that time she would remark, "You know Steven, you and Jan have something that none of my friends with all their possessions have. You have peace with God—and money cannot buy it!"

But in the meantime, our ministry was to begin with a cross-country trip. The ministry could not provide a van for us at that time, and we really couldn't afford one ourselves. We sold our little Fiat as a down payment and then went looking for a loan. I explained to our banker that God was calling us into a full-time ministry, and we needed to borrow $10,000 to purchase a new van. When he found out we would be receiving $400 a month salary each *and* that we were leaving the state to begin touring, he laughed. Despite our good credit standing, he—and several other bankers after him—declined the loan. They just couldn't see that God's provision for those who follow His leading as a valid basis for the loan!

Yet, the day before we left Tacoma, a dealer agreed to write us the loan. He promptly sold it to the bank that had first refused us. (Nine months later, we had paid off the entire loan. Fifteen months later, the van was stolen right off the streets of Queens, New York. But three days before it was stolen, a supporter had given Jews for Jesus $10,000 to buy a new van. Indeed, God does provide!)

We set out in our new van and headed for Chicago. There we joined the rest of the Jews for Jesus for an intense outreach called a witnessing campaign.

That particular campaign, called Operation Birthday Cake, coincided with the bicentennial celebration of the founding of our country. Jan and I were assigned to a team of people who traveled to Philadelphia, New York City, Washington D.C. and Boston. We participated in what was to be one of the longest witnessing campaigns in the history of Jews for Jesus! When it was over, Jan and I went on a tour from August, 1976 to May, 1977. We simply drove wherever we could get a hearing, setting up church presentations with whomever was willing to have us. We visited places like Black Duck, Minnesota; Lemmon, South Dakota and George, Washington. These travels provided us the opportunity to do evangelism in cities where Jews for Jesus did not have an outreach and to make friends and build a base of support for our ministry. To this day, some of the friends we made on that tour continue to uphold us.

On the last Sunday of January, 1977, I scheduled an evening presentation at a church in Richland, Washington. We prayed that my parents would come and hear our presentation of Christ in the Passover and Jewish Gospel music.

They had invited us to visit them before the service. It was Super Bowl Sunday, and it was the middle of the third quarter when we arrived. It was cold outside, but it seemed even colder inside their home that afternoon. It was the only time I can ever remember that my mother didn't offer us a thing to eat. It was then and there that my father made his announcement: "You broke with Jewish tradition by believing in Jesus as your Messiah. It has become obvious that this is not a passing fad, since you have dedicated your life to telling others what you believe. Therefore, we do not want to have anything further to do with you. *Do not write, do not call, and do not visit us—ever again!* If you write, we will throw away your letters. If you call, we will hang up. And if you come to visit, we will close the door on you."

We left with tears in our eyes and drove to a nearby restaurant. I was a missionary to my people, yet I could not reach those I loved most. That evening service was extremely emotional for me. It was the first of many nights when I asked others to join me in praying for my parents: *"Lord, raise up someone else who is not ashamed of the Gospel to reach out to my parents."* The wonderful people of that church shared our pain that night, and many continued praying for my family. A few people from that congregation still write to inquire after my parents.

In May of 1977, Jan and I were assigned to the New York branch of Jews for Jesus. We rented an apartment in Flushing, a neighborhood in Queens, and began reaching out to the Jewish community there. An ancillary part of our ministry is helping Christians who want to witness to Jewish friends. In the spring of 1978, Jan and I were invited to speak at a small church in East Brunswick, New Jersey. It was a Saturday afternoon meeting, and we were to take ten minutes to make our presentation and answer a few questions. I recall wondering, "Why are we driving all this way to speak to a handful of people for ten minutes?" (Time would tell. Nine years later, I received a letter from a woman who had attended that 1978 meeting. She tracked us down to let us know that a Jewish family that she had witnessed to as a result of that meeting had all come to faith in Jesus. The entire family had just been baptized and joined their church.)

One of my assignments in 1978 was to do weekly outreach on the campus of Queens College in Queens, Long Island. This commuter campus had a population of more than 10,000 Jewish students. Our first event was an open air concert by the Liberated Wailing Wall. A sizable crowd gathered; some were stirred up with interest and others with hostility toward the gospel. I met some of the believers on the campus who wanted to learn about ministry to the Jewish community. We became friends and spent the school year together doing various activities: broadsiding, seminars, films and open discussions on the messiahship of Jesus.

It didn't take long for some of the Jewish students to organize opposition to our evangelism. Sometimes it took less than ten minutes for a crowd to surrounded me, taunting, tearing up literature and generally trying to stop others from hearing what I had to say.

Every week, I felt a sense of uneasiness, sometimes even dread as I prepared myself for yet another attempt at outreach. Yet, without fail, the moment I stepped onto the campus, peace flooded my heart—a peace that passed all understanding. God was in control. I was just doing my duty, and that duty was to care, to pray and to spend two hours a week on that Queens College campus, trying to reach out to the students.

The day the Holocaust commemoration took place at Queens College, I did not wear my usual Jews for Jesus T-shirt, and I didn't bring our usual gospel broadsides. I came in street clothes and brought dozens of copies of a now out-of-print Jews for Jesus booklet written to denounce anti-Semitism. Even without the T-shirt and tracts, a near riot broke out. Three security guards flanked me, as more than 400 people surrounded us. Their anger rose to near boiling, but Jews for Jesus had trained me to respond only if people speak one at a time, and amazingly, they responded when I insisted that they take turns speaking.

A voice shouted from the midst of the crowd, and I told the man who was trying to break in that he would have to wait. He turned out to be the president of the college. He'd heard the commotion, left his office and was attempting to bring the campus back to normalcy. When he identified himself and asked me to accompany him to his office, I knew he was trying to diffuse the situation and remove me from possible danger.

Yet, I had only been on the campus for forty-five minutes. I was startled to hear myself say, "Dr. Segal, I would be more than happy to come to your office. However, I need to stay here a full two hours just as I always have over the past few months. I would be happy to make an appointment so we can talk later." Much to my surprise, he stayed and served as a sounding board for the next hour and a quarter. Reporters from all five student papers were there, and the following week their front pages covered the "event" and raised the issue of Jews believing in Jesus as the Messiah.

The articles continued throughout the year. Most were distortions of who we were and what we were saying, but some were fair. The opposition actually boosted our cause and raised the issue of the Messiah even higher. The articles and editorials drew many of those sitting on the fence into the discussion.

I didn't see one person come to faith in Jesus while I was on the campus. A few years later at a Jews for Jesus event, a young lady introduced herself to me as a former Queens College student. She had watched me from afar and had observed all the opposition and commotion. She never approached me, never even took one of my tracts, but she did pick up literature that others had flung to the ground—and she read it. That literature spurred her on to question her Christian friends. They presented the Gospel—and she received God's gift of salvation.

In August of 1978, Jan and I were transferred to Omaha to teach personal evangelism and to take classes at Omaha Lutheran Bible School. I wondered why we were leaving the heart of the largest Jewish population in the world to move to a place that had maybe 5,000 Jewish people. However, the Lord used our time there. We learned from some godly professors and built relationships.

We returned to New York City in 1980; only this time, we were a threesome. We were happy to be back in New York and happy with our healthy baby boy, Micha.

Over the next decade, Jan and I had all kinds of adventures and opportunities to serve God through the ministry of Jews for Jesus. We ministered for a time in Toronto, Canada, as well as in Boston, Massachusetts.

Our lives were busy and full, and our family grew! Micha was joined by Sarah, Noah, Seth and eventually, Elizabeth. I wished my parents could see them all, but our occasional attempts to break the wall of silence always met swift rejection. Then, in 1990, my brother told me the news.

My father had cancer. He told my brother that he had no intention of seeking medical treatment of any kind. Dad had seen his father and sister suffer grievously through surgical and chemical treatments for their cancers, and he would not do the same. When the pain became unbearable, he intended to end his own life.

I'd had no direct communication with my parents since 1977. I'd been praying for fourteen years that the Lord would raise up someone else to reach them with the gospel. That prayer became an urgent plea because my father was running out of time.

I set up a chain of prayer through Jews for Jesus staff and supporters. I invited some of my closest supporters and friends to write a short note or a postcard to my parents letting them know they were praying. I never knew when a phone call would come, telling me of my father's fate.

I'll never forget May 22, 1990. I'd just finished speaking at a pastors' conference on Cape Cod, near Boston. I had urged people to involve themselves in reaching out to all and asked them to pray specifically for my family: for reconciliation, healing and, most importantly, for their salvation. The moment I closed with prayer someone strode forward to hand me an urgent message from Dennis. He had tracked me down to tell me that our father had swallowed a bottle of pills in an attempt to take his life that morning. Dad failed in that attempt, but time was running out. I drove straight to the Boston airport and flew across country.

Ten hours later I was in my hometown of Pasco, Washington. Dennis met me at the airport with a message from my parents, telling me to get on the next plane to Boston because I was not welcome in their home. All they wanted from me was that I leave them alone.

Well, there were no planes out that night, so Dennis and I went to a motel. We talked, prayed and even laughed as we reminisced about our childhood. The following day, I knew I couldn't take the next plane to Boston. I had to try to see my father. Eternity was hanging in the balance.

I called my old friend, Alan Rither. I met him at his office, and he took time off to bring me to his home where we prayed together. And at 4:00 P.M. on May 23, 1990, I did something I hadn't done in fourteen years: I rang my parents' doorbell. The lights were out, the front gate was padlocked, and there were no vehicles in the driveway. I assumed that they had chosen to leave until after I had returned to Boston. Still, I rang the bell, knowing I had to try. Even though there was no response, I stood there. A couple of minutes passed, and the garage door swung open. Out walked my brother, looking utterly mystified. "I don't understand it, with all that has happened in the past, they have decided to see you now!"

I entered into the living room, and my father struggled out of his chair. Cancer had ravaged his body. I remembered Dad with jet black hair and eyes that danced with merriment. Now he was aged beyond his years and wracked with pain. No words were spoken as I crossed the room. With tears in my eyes and his, we hugged for the longest time. God had answered my prayer for reconciliation.

I can't tell the story without thinking about the parable of the Prodigal Son. In our case, it was more like the Prodigal Father! And the fatted calf? Well, we didn't keep livestock in the Cohen home, but we had the next best thing—Chinese food! The restaurant that we used to go to when I was young was still in business, so I ordered a take-out feast.

I offered a brief prayer of thanksgiving for the food and for the reconciliation and asked for healing for Dad. When I finished, I couldn't miss the tears streaming down my mother's face. Prayers were not a part of our family life, but she was greatly touched by this one.

We were a family again! We sat around the dining room table, and I told of the many cities in which we'd lived, the adventures and, of course, I showed pictures of our five beautiful children. I told them what a wonderful mother Jan is and how Micha had started to learn Hebrew in anticipation of his *bar mitzvah*. I described how we light Sabbath candles in our home and celebrate Jewish festivals like Passover, Rosh Hashannah and Yom Kippur, and, I explained, at the same time our children were enrolled in classes at our church.

My mother was astonished. Her comment was, "You know what Steven? It seems like your faith in Jesus has made you *even more* Jewish!"

I replied, "Mom, if Jesus *is* the Jewish Messiah, what could be more Jewish than following Him? If He is not the Messiah, then even the Gentiles are wasting their time following Him." My parents did not demonstrate any openness to the gospel message. However, they did comment on the thoughtfulness of more than thirty friends and supporters of mine who had written to let my parents know of their prayers concerning my father's illness.

By the end of our visit, Mom and Dad said I was welcome to come back, but they did not want me to bring up the issue of Jesus in their presence.

It was clear that Dad was out of the woods for the time being, so I returned to Boston. My prayers for another person to witness to him continued. Over the next six months, we were able to have what seemed to me like little miracles—phone calls with my parents. We could talk about anything, except what was most important—Y'shua.

Jan and I were preparing to move to Ft. Lauderdale right after Thanksgiving, 1990, and it was about that time that Dad decided to go into a hospital. He chose St. Vincent's Hospital in Portland, Oregon, where I had been born. My cousin was working there and could help him get the care he needed. I flew out to see him one last time.

I spent four days with my father. He was on a morphine drip to control the pain, but other than this, there was little that could be done. I helped him shave, shared meals with him and we spoke of what life would be like for the family after he died. Still, he would not hear from me about the life-giving message of Jesus.

I returned to Boston, where I had to arrange for our move to Florida and work on our annual conference of Jewish believers in Jesus, which we call an Ingathering.

We arrived at the Ingathering, where I received an emergency message—but it was not about my father. It was just one week before we were to move, and the mortgage for the people who were buying our Boston home fell apart. Meanwhile, we had put *all* our available cash into a non-refundable deposit on a home in Florida.

I was convinced that only the Lord could intervene in this set of circumstances: my father was near death, we were in the midst of a move, the mortgage brokers for our new home would not approve us until they had written evidence that our house in Boston was sold and if we didn't get our mortgage within two weeks, we would lose our down payment, which was basically everything. Yet, I felt a total peace in the midst of everything.

We returned from the Ingathering and finished packing in preparation for the movers. They still were scheduled to come the day after Thanksgiving so we could move to Florida, where we might or might not have a home.

On Thanksgiving morning, at 1:30 A.M., Jan and I were jarred awake by the telephone. The only reason I could imagine for someone to call at that hour was to give us bad news. I was immediately relieved to hear that it wasn't my brother, but rather it was my cousin, Susan.

Susan had come to faith in Jesus in the late 1980s. She and I sometimes talked about the Lord and what God was doing in her life. She and my Dad were close, so I occasionally asked her to speak to him about Jesus. Susan was somewhat apprehensive; she didn't know what to say or how to go about it. I asked her to trust God and simply tell Dad what God had done in her life, explaining the simple gospel message. It was hard to know if she would follow through on my request.

It was the early hours of Thanksgiving Day when Susan called to tell me that she had done it—she told the gospel to my father. She repeated her message word for word so I could hear it. "Uncle Bobbie," she had said, "God loves you very much. He sent Jesus, our Messiah, to die for you so that you could have eternal life. Wouldn't you want to receive God's free gift of eternal life?"

Her voice dropped down to a whisper, "And do you know what, Steven? He said, 'Yes.' I prayed with him right there in the hospital room to receive God's gift of salvation!"

"Praise the Lord," was all I could say, and I was so overwhelmed that it's a wonder I could even say that much!

The next morning I had my last conversation with Dad. I called him to rejoice in his coming to faith and to let him know how much I loved him and how glad I was to know that I would see him in heaven. He was so very tired, thus the conversation was brief. At the end of our call, Dad assured me that though he only a few days left on earth, he knew he would spend eternity with the Lord. I was so very thankful on that Thanksgiving Day!

The following day the movers came and took away all our belongings, yet we still had no place to go. After the movers left, I took a shower, which is why I didn't hear the phone ring. But even with the running water, I heard the children shouting and jumping up and down.

The call had been from the real estate agent. He had no idea how, but the buyer had managed to get a new mortgage application approved in just four days! The sale of our home would go through, a couple of days late, but it would go through in time for our closing in Florida. God took care of it all!

During the three-day journey from Boston to our next ministry station in Ft. Lauderdale, we were out of touch with the world. When we arrived in Ft. Lauderdale, I called my mother to let her know that we were safe. Her first words were, "Have you spoken with your brother yet?" I hadn't. She hesitated, then said, "I had hoped he would be the one to let you know that your father died on Monday."

Mother was doing her best to maintain her composure. "Your father did not want a funeral service. I told him that since we were not religious, I would honor his wishes." It was then that I told mother about Dad's commitment to Christ. Her response was, "If that helped him in his last days, then so be it." Later on, an attending nurse who was at my father's bedside when he died told me, "Minutes before your father died, he sat straight up in bed with a glorious smile on his face and said, 'I'm starting my journey home to God now.' Then he lay down in peace and entered into the presence of the Lord."

We closed on the house in Ft. Lauderdale the next afternoon. With keys in hand, I called the movers to let them know where to bring the furniture. They gave me the "bad news"—they had lost our furniture. I'm sure those movers never expected my response. I just laughed. After all we'd been through, the misplaced furniture hardly seemed devastating. I told the movers we had sleeping bags and cooking utensils, and when they found our things, they should give us a call.

We quickly settled into our work, thankful for all that God had done in bringing us to that point.

I had once dreamed of becoming a lawyer, but God gave me the privilege of telling people that though we have broken His laws, He has provided a gracious means of reconciliation. Who could ask for more? And oh yes, even to this day I find confirmation that I am doing what the Lord wants. Sometimes I'll look up as I am driving late at night, I'll wonder…and the streetlight will flicker almost as if to remind me of how God has been so real, so personal in my life.

If you are not a believer in Jesus yet, please ask God to show you if it is true that our Messiah has come. Be willing to consider the evidence of Scripture. Y'shua has stood the test of time for nearly 2,000 years, and I am fully persuaded that any Jew or Gentile who truly desires to know God's truth will discover it in the person of Jesus.

If you are already a believer, please don't be afraid to tell those who so deeply need what you have found in Jesus. God used the persistence of one caring, praying Christian to bring me to my Messiah. My prayer is that through you, many will also come to know what we know: peace through the Prince of Peace.

"For I am not ashamed of the gospel of Christ, for it is the power of God to salvation for everyone who believes, for the Jew first and also for the Greek." (Romans 1:16)

Steve Cohen has a B.A. in sociology from the University of Washington and an M.A. in missiology with concentration in Jewish evangelism/Judaic studies from the Fuller School of World Missions in Pasadena, California.

He says, "It is with much gratitude for all that I have received through caring Christian friends that I hope to encourage others to continue reaching out with the Good News of Jesus to Jews as well as Gentiles. I find tremendous encouragement in 1 Corinthians 15:58, and I hope that you will, too: 'Therefore, my beloved brethren, be steadfast, immovable, always abounding in the work of the Lord, knowing that your labor is not in vain in the Lord.' "

For information about Jewish Evangelism, write to:

Jews for Jesus
60 Haight Street
San Francisco, CA 94102
415-864-2600
FAX: 415-552-8325

For a catalog of messianic books and products, write to:

Purple Pomegranate Productions
80 Page Street
San Francisco, CA 94102